Mal and Mag

Malmag is the common name of the Philippine Tarsier. In this story, two playful tarsiers "Mal and Mag" discover that their homes are being cut down by the selfish woodcutters. They ran away from the site to seek new shelter.

Were they able to find a new home? Do we still have Philippine Tarsiers today?

*When this book was created in 1995, very little efforts have been done to save the Philippine Tarsier. Fortunately in 1997, the **Philippine Tarsier Foundation** implemented the **Philippine Tarsier Conservation Program** and in 2009, the **Tarsius Project** began with tarsier research and conservation.*

We must work together by promoting environmental awareness, eliciting respect, and demonstrating our appreciation for the Philippine Wildlife. Moreover, we should also continue to conserve our land, the shelter to our endangered species.

Si Mal at si Mag
Mal and Mag

Written by: **Maria Luisa Dy-Liacco Marin**
Illustrated by: **Jason Moss**

Sa masukal na kagubatan ng lungsod Tagbilaran
may dalawang Tarsier
matalik na magkaibigan.

Si Mal na mahilig kumain ng mga batang ibon
si Mag naman ang gawain ay manghuli ng hipon.

In the deep and thick forest of Tagbilaran City, there lived two tarsiers, namely, Mal and Mag. They are the best of friends.

Mal is very fond of eating young birds, while Mag is too busy catching shrimps.

Sila ang isa sa pinakamaliit
na primado sa buong mundo
isang dangkal lang ang haba
mga anim na pulgada.

Pagsapit ng dilim sila'y
maliksing-maliksi
ngunit sa umaga'y tahimik
halos hindi umiimik.

Tarsiers are one of the
smallest primates in the
whole world. Their size is
about a hand's length, which
is about six inches long.

By sunset, as twilight begins
to engulf the day, these tiny
creatures are active and
lively, but come sunrise, they
could be hardly heard at all.

Dumating and isang araw
madaling-madali
ang dalawa'y napadalaw
sa kanilang mga kasapi.

Palukso-lukso ng dala-
dalawang talampakan
umaakyat, bumababa sa mga
kapunuan.

A day came when the two
friends excitedly paid a visit
to their other friends.

They jumped and hopped,
climbing up and down the
trees with gay abandon.

Nagtataguan sa mga palumpong nag-uunahan makahuli ng tipaklong.

They played hide and seek, and raced with one another in catching grasshoppers.

Simple lang ang kanilang
buhay, masaya at matiwasay
ilag lang sa ahas at pusa
at baka sila'y mamatay.

Life for tarsiers is simple,
happy and peaceful. The
only threats to their lives are
snakes and cats which they
have to avoid at all times.

Nung minsan ay may nakita ang dalawang magkaibigan mga taong may dala-dalang iba't-ibang kagamitan.

One day, the two friends were surprised to see people carrying with them different sorts of equipment.

Nagtaka si Mal at si Mag
dahil sila'y pinagmamasdan
pati ang mga tirahan
na kanilang pinapasukan.

Hindi sila huminto
sa kanilang paglalaro
ngunit mayroong kaba
silang nadama.

Mal and Mag wondered why
these men kept looking at
them and their homes.

This did not stop them
from playing but it gave
them reason to be nervous.

Nag-umpisang maghiwalay
sa bukang-liwayway
si Mal at si Mag nang may
narinig silang ingay.

Grrrrrrrrrrrrrrr....................
Grrrrrrrrrrrrrrr....................
Eeeeeeeeeeeeeek....................
Baaaaaaaaaaaaag....................
Baaaaaaaaaaaaag....................

At the break of dawn, as Mal
and Mag were parting ways,
they heard loud sounds
like...

Grrrrrrrrrrrrrrr....................
Grrrrrrrrrrrrrrr....................
Eeeeeeeeeeeeeek....................
Baaaaaaaaaaaaag....................
Baaaaaaaaaaaaag....................

Lalo lang nanlaki ang
kanilang mga mata
tinakpan ng mabuti
ang maninipis nilang tainga.

Their big eyes became much
bigger as they tightly
covered their thin-layered
ears.

Matatapang na mantotroso
unti-unting tinatabasan
ng walang pag-alinlangan at
respeto sa kanilang tirahan.

Isa-isang bumagsak ang mga
punong-kahoy
pati na rin ang pangarap
na ang buhay nila'y
magpatuloy.

What they saw were fearless
woodcutters, slowly cutting
down their homes without
hesitation and respect.

As the trees fell one by one,
so did their shattered
dreams of a happy and
longer life.

Dahil dito sa kagubatan
nakasalalaly ang kanilang buhay
kung wala ng masisilungan
kalusuga'y mapapabayaan.

Higit na nalungkot
ang magkaibigan sa nangyari
" kami'y natatakot! "
ang matinis nilang huni.

The forest means so much to their existence. It is a lifeline they cling on to. Without any shelter, their health would be greatly compromised.

This tragedy greatly saddened the two friends. "We are afraid!", was all they could mutter in their high pitched chirp.

Kaya't tumakbo sa kalayuan
ang magkaibigan
hahanap ng bagong tirahan
na hindi pa natutuklasan.

It is for this reason that the
two friends ran to a far away
place in order to find a new
home that has never been
explored.

Nakahanap si Mal at si Mag
ng bagong tirahan.
Sumama rin ang ibang mga
hayop sa kanilang bago at
tahimik na kagubatan.

Marami pang mga hayop
ang nasa ganitong kalagayan
sila'y ating tulungan
ILIGTAS ANG KAGUBATAN!

Mal and Mag found a new
home. They were soon
joined by their other friends
in their new and
undiscovered forest.

Many other animals are in
the same predicament.
Let us all help them.
SAVE THE FOREST!

Updates on the Philippine Tarsier:

The **Philippine Tarsier Foundation** is an organization that has promised to help conserve and preserve the Philippine Tarsiers. This Foundation has dedicated 8.4 hectares of secondary growth forest as its main conservation area. This vast area, now called the **Philippine Tarsier and Wildlife Sanctuary,** located in Canapnapan, Corella, Bohol in the Philippines, holds approximately one hundred (100) live Tarsiers. (2015, July 21). The Tarsier Sanctuary. Retrieved from www.tarsierfoundation.org

Tarsius Project has managed to captivate two tarsiers, a male tarsier named Julius and a female tarsier named Nina. Julius and Nina are the first pair of tarsiers in the conservation and breeding center. This is part of the project's attempt to breed more tarsiers in the Philippines. Moreover, Tarsius Project has been involved in disseminating information about Tarsiers nationwide and conducting research work that will serve as a basis for future conservation activities. Milada. (2015, July 18). The Tarsius Project. Retrieved from www.tarsiusproject.org

For more information on the plight of the Philippine Tarsiers, you may visit the websites mentioned above. This will also give you the opportunity to volunteer and save the Philippine Tarsiers.

Maria Luisa Dy-Liacco Marin

This book was created way back in 1995 when the author chanced upon a Philippine newspaper article entitled "World's smallest monkey on verge of extinction". To fulfill one requirement for her Master's class and as a professor at the University of the Philippines-Child Development Center, Louie took into consideration the urgent desire among the faculty to Filipinize the curriculum. Hence, she wrote this book for her young students then.

At present, Louie resides in the United States of America with her family. She continues to teach and touch lives of young children.

Jason Moss

Jason illustrated this book at the age of 20. He was a 3rd year college student then at the University of Santo Tomas where he majored in Advertising. At present, Jason is a successful and much sought-after illustrator of storybooks and a professor at the Ateneo de manila. He is an accomplished painter and has held more than 20 one-man shows showcasing his beautiful art works. He is pursuing his Master's degree at the University of the Philippines, College of Fine Arts. He has won top awards for his contribution in children's literature.